Copyright © Allen Mbengeranwa 2014

Your Small Restaurant: The Bistro (Café/Diner) Practical Business Plan

ISBN: 978-1-291-99889-4

Disclaimer and Legal Notice

While all attempts have been made to verify the information provided in this publication, neither the Author nor the Publisher assumes any responsibility for errors, omissions or contradictory interpretation of the subject matter herein. This publication is not intended for use as a source of any form of legal, financial, emotional, personal or accounting advice. The content is not a substitute or replacement of sound professional, insured advice. Please make up your own mind or engage the services of an individual or organisation willing to accept the responsibility which the author and publisher clearly will not, under any and all possible circumstances. The publisher wishes to let it be known and accepted that the information and illustrations contained herein may be subject to different geographical rules, regulations and laws. All users are advised to verify and determine what local rules, regulations and laws that their independent restaurant or business may be subject to. The reader or purchaser of this work assumes responsibility for the use of these materials and information. Please accept and understand all local official and professional guides, rules, laws and regulations that govern your chosen business activity.

Allen Mbengeranwa

DRAFT VERSION ONE

CONFIDENTIAL

COPY No…..

The Bistro
Café/Diner

CONFIDENTIALITY AGREEMENT

The reader acknowledges that the information provided in this business plan is confidential; therefore, the reader agrees not to disclose it without the express permission of Allen, creator, owner and facilitator of The Bistro concept.

It is acknowledged by the reader that information to be furnished in this business plan is in all respects confidential in nature, other than information which is the public domain through other means and that any disclosure or use of the same by reader, or associates, may cause serious harm or damage to The Bistro concept and business venture.

Upon request, this document is to be immediately returned to Allen.

This is a Business Plan; it does not imply an offering of securities.

Table of Contents: - The Bistro (Café/Diner)

Table of Figures 4

Executive Summary 5

Background/Business History 9

Products/service 10

The Market & Marketing 13

The Product Plan 32

Resource Plan 37

Competition 40

Pricing 41

Premises 59

Operating and Control Systems 60

Contingency Plans 67

Capital Expenditure 70

Staffing Requirements 74

Legal Aspects 75

Financial Information 77

Appendices 84

Table of Figures

Figure 1 Service Plan 12
Figure 2 Service Delivery Model 27
Figure 3 Restaurant Equipment Inventory 37
Figure 4 Operating and Control System 60
Figure 5 Sales Monitoring System 63
Figure 6 The Bistro Start-Up Costs 72
Figure 7 The Bistro Capital Requirement 73
Figure 8 Financial Requirements 78
Figure 9 Financial Assumptions 79
Figure 10 Break Even 80
Figure 11 Cash Flow Forecast Summary 82

Executive Summary

The origins of the word 'bistro' are disputed. Some say it was introduced by the Russians after the invasion of Paris in 1814, as they shouted '***Bystro!***' (Meaning 'quickly!'), at waiters in busy cafés. Some argue that it evolved from Parisian slang of the time, and others trace the term to a northern dialect. But wherever the word began, the bistro experience has not strayed too far from its roots.

Our authentic bistro fare is the essence of the restaurant. It is honest, fresh and satisfying food prepared to order. The menu is not complicated. Bistro food is real food, for real people.

The dishes are of simple up-to-date versions of good, old fashioned food. Our ingredients are basic; preparations are simple and emphasis health benefits.

Bistro food started in home kitchens and bistro is about making the most of ingredients and it's about value for money.

Our bistro concept uses our appetite for authentic flavours and satisfying meals, which gives our bistro meals enduring appeal.

Our bistro is more than just cuisine. It's a way of life.

The Bistro takes advantage of the location and available premises to develop its business model. The location is in area of predominantly residential accommodation with some business and offices. The area is close to the M8 and is parallel to Great Western road.

The business' model it to develop the café and continue to offer breakfast services and introduce lunch and dinner services. The location of the café dictates the need for a low volume, high margin business model that focuses on students and the surrounding business location during the day and local residents at night.

The menus are designed to highlight the available resources and facilities. The café will continue to offer traditional breakfasts as well as introducing business specific items like eggs Benedict and Eggs St. Charles for breakfast. The concept is to add value to the location and differentiate the service from nearby competitors and appeal to a wider range of customers.

The evening menu will include classic bistro meals such as mussels a la bouillabaisse (mussels with fennel, tomato, garlic and saffron), steak frites and others. This will suit the café and local area.

The restaurant/café industry continues to grow as the standard of living increase in general and specific to the West End of Glasgow. The decline in sales for fast food restaurants has led to increases in sales for healthy eating and quality conscious eateries.

The location was once a fruit and vegetable shop that was converted into a class three café and has not been operating for a few years. The last tenant operated the location as a Turkish Community centre. It has been said that the location benefits from a recent refit and the capacity for 24 covers.

On initial inspection, there are services connected to the site. These have not been professionally tested, but a visual inspection indicates they are working. The kitchen and dining area are located on the ground floor with the toilets and storage located at basement level. The two levels are connected by a spiral staircase.

There are potential options to develop a catering and delivery service for the business. There is also potential to **[PROPRIETARY INFORMATION REMOVED]**

Finances

The forecasts indicate that we will be able to break even, from an operational perspective. Our sales have been forecast by various market research techniques including the custom at the local competitors and deducing estimations. We anticipate sales of £51,800.00 and a residual cash inflow figure of at least £1,681.92. The business has a tight cash flow model, as do all restaurants. This is because there will be no lines of credit available from suppliers and the majority of bills will be paid monthly. This will require the use of software that is able to forecast and present the situation on a regular basis.

The business model needs an estimate of £10,335.36 to fund the start up. This includes the structural work, purchase of fixed assets and fixtures and fittings. Like all restaurants, the majority of the funding is allocated to the kitchen area. The temptation to use second hand goods has been avoided as the new equipment comes with 12 month warranties. Breakdowns have been known to sink restaurants when there's no warranty.

The total start-up funding needed is £10,335.36 and the working capital of £4,000.00. These figures will be significantly lower as the income from the business will be used to fund operations.

The capital repayment is estimated at £2,067.24 per year. This means that the loan capital repayments are estimated at 20% in year one. An interest rate of 8% has been adopted. The payments have been estimated at £826.80 for the first year. This is over and above the actual repayments as a higher principle has been used to calculate the payments.

This business plan is the first version and has many items omitted to reduce the bulk. These include recruitment forms and other administration material.

Furthermore, the business model needs to be refined with all possibilities having been explored. It is a difficult location and schemes are needed to build the business and make it sustainable and profitable. This will enable a Fair Maintainable Trade to be assessed and monitored.

It is hoped that more experienced partners will be sort for the business model and operation.

Background/Business History

Personal History

A graduate of Accounting and Finance from the University of Wales, Bangor 2004. Previous employment includes a position as an Account Assistant at the Institute Of Actuaries. Business training was mainly gained from training provided by the Welsh Development Agency through local agencies between 2001 and 2004.

Products/service

Product/Service description

The Bistro (Café/Diner) will offer a breakfast service in the mornings from 7am to 11am. This will be offering an option of the traditional breakfast, traditional Scottish breakfast and more modern offerings such as eggs Benedict, free range scrambled eggs with Salmon soldiers on brown bread, eggs St. Charles, premium forest ham with figs plus continental breakfast options. There will be a sit in and take away facility available for this breakfast service. There is nothing revolutionary or innovative about this service as it is already used by JD Weatherspoons pubs, McDonald's restaurant the local café competition on Woodlands road.

The bistro will also offer a bistro menu between 12 am and 8pm. This menu will be mostly French inspired with seasonal variations. As the café is small, in true bistro style there will be a set menu comprising starters, mains, deserts and sides. The menu will be that of a typical French bistro with mains of *steak frites* (Streak and home-cut fries with shallot butter), *cotes de porc charcuterie* (Pork chops with piquant sauce), ratatouille, a selection of vegetable gratins, braised red cabbage with chestnuts and apples.

As there is no license in place, The Bistro will offer corkage of £3 per person and £4 for couples. This will also serve as a fantastic marketing ploy and increase the volume of cost conscious customers.

The café is planned to develop in such a way that also allows for a catering service to be introduced for the local businesses. This is aimed at increasing revenue and enhancing the location of the restaurant by taking advantage of the lucrative business market, and not just domestic local residents. The catering service will be formed of a lunch section of baguette filled rolls and salads and the catering section will include canapés, aimed at business meetings.

The diagram bellow illustrates the nature of the Service Plan that I intend to use:

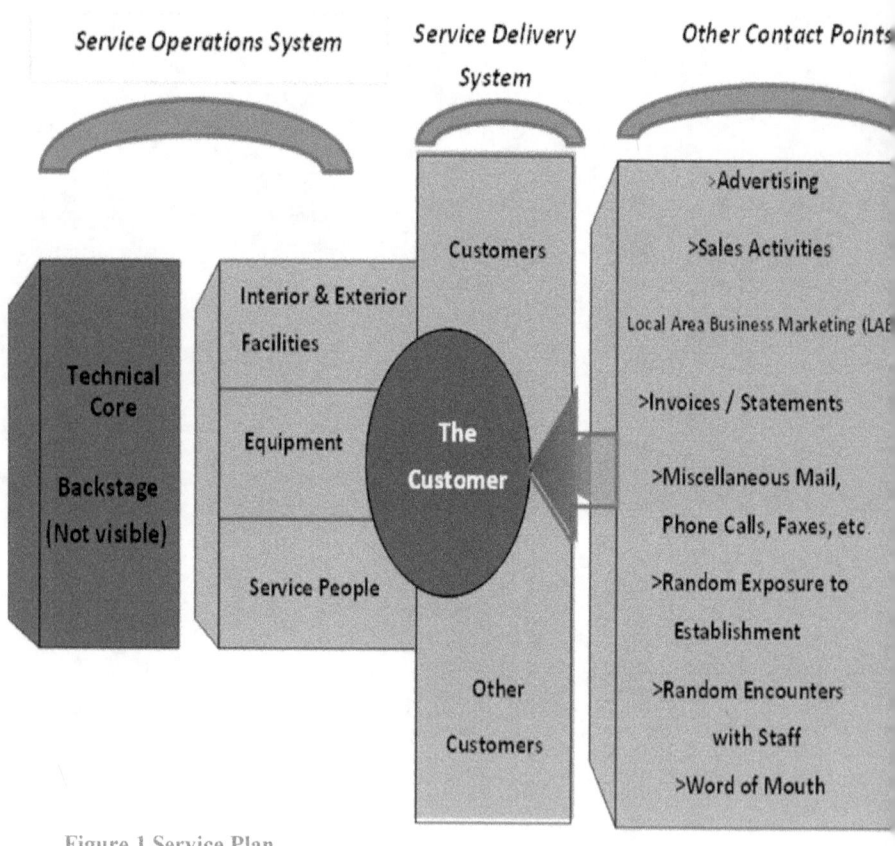

Figure 1 Service Plan

The Market & Marketing

Market research

The market research was made up of desk based research as well as field (Hit the road!) research. The former included visits to the Mitchell Library business centre for newspapers, market reports, directories, government(especially local council) information, trade information, trade press publications.

The latter included visiting local competitors, using the Yellow Pages and among other activities, visiting other restaurant concepts.

Professional market research reports define restaurants as eating places supplying meals for consumption on the premises. The market includes both licensed and unlicensed premises. The market is defined to cover 'restaurant meals' only and expenditure on drinks is not usually included in the market sizes.

The market for eating out is mostly split up into pre-family and post-family diners although family dining is also available but tends to be avoided by the other split areas.

The market sectors are divided into the following:
1. Fast food
2. Pubs and hotels
3. Asian (traditional)
4. Pizza/pasta
5. Chicken
6. Roadside
7. British café's/ restaurants e.g steakhouses, unlicensed café's
8. Continental and other restaurants

It is said that within the seven sectors, the general characteristic is fragmentation across independent owners. There is also polarisation between large and small companies as the independents are combined with the presents of large chains of national and multinational branded restaurants – notably in fast food, but also in pub-restaurants.

The advertising spending in the restaurant market is dominated by the multinational chains. For the year ending 2005, McDonald's and KFC accounted for 60% of all restaurant advertising. Apart from fast food, pizza hut spends on average £7.4 million. Whitbread, which owns Pizza Hut and other brands, spent the most non-fast food money in total. Of greater importance to this concept is that the smaller independents spent on average, £1,200.00 per campaign.

The £1,200.00 for individual small scale restaurants is said to reflect the use of cheap but effective local advertising media. Radio is said to be sometimes used, but the predominant outlet to the public is local newspapers, which may review local restaurants and certainly provide pages of listings for restaurants to visit.

The Market

A restaurant is defined by Keynote as an eating place supplying meals for consumption on the premises.

The market include both licensed and unlicensed eateries and covers 'restaurant meals' only income expenditure on drinks is not usually included in the market sizes.

Eating out is generally higher among the pre-family and post-family years possibly due to the increased time and available funds.

The industry accepted division of market sectors in the restaurant trade is as follows:
1. Fast food – eat in meals only
2. Pubs and hotels
3. Asian (traditional)
4. Pizza/Pasta
5. Chicken
6. Roadside
7. British café's/restaurants e.g steakhouses and unlicensed cafés
8. Continental and other restaurants

Measurability

The City of Glasgow has a population of approximately 630,000 persons which is substantially increased with the inclusion of outlying suburbs, new towns and a large student population, estimated at around 135,000. Glasgow is also one of the main leisure entertainment centres in the UK and is ranked second only to London as a retail location

This information shows the size and nature of the restaurant catchment area, from which the vast majority of our customers will arise. It is feasible to assume that these numbers have since increased with the advent of inward migration from the European Union and the English speaking world at large. This is a reasonable assumption as the area is of lower income than other Great British cities.

Woodlands road, Hillhead, is close to Byres road and therefore part of the affluent West End of Glasgow. The outlet is also close to Charing Cross and St. Georges underground stations. There is a small business community (by volume) around this area including the Barclays UK stock broking division. The area is also has a junction with the M8.

Accessibility

We will be able to communicate with these customers in a number of ways. We will be able to produce leaflets to deliver to the households and businesses, as a form of communication to educate potential customers of our location and services.

We will also produce advertisements in the local papers which include The West End mail and The Evening Standard, at a later stage so as to reduce start-up costs. Nonetheless, we will have public relations activities underway for editorials and listings.

We will also aim to market our services through local hair dressers and beauty clinics. This will involve us offering 10% of to the clients of the hair dressers. Of these, there is Toni and Guy on woodlands road and more on Sauchiehall Street.

We will also access the local market by offering 10% of to the emergency services, blue lights.

We will access the public sector employees by offering a free meal for two to a nominated individual. This individual will be nominated by the human resources departments with one from the Local Authority and another from the local NHS trust.

Size

This represents a large proportion of people likely to purchase our services, and that of competitors. It is not possible to establish the exact number of people who eat out and how often they do. We aim to attract 7,176 diners per annum. . This is the figure that will be needed on the average spend in order to make a minimal profit. The average spend has been assumed to be £10 per head.

For the general market, Keynote reports that the 'cash rich and time poor customers' with an increase in disposable income are encouraging more discretionary spending on eating out and other leisure activities. The average household – not necessarily a family spent £29.10 per week on meals and drinks outside the house, including takeaways, (but not drink) brought home. Of greater importance is the fact that the sit down meals accounted for £11.20 of this spending, representing a (38.5% share).

Given the location of the restaurant in the affluent West End, this figure will be higher and with covers of up to 34 will lead to higher revenues and customer bases.

The decline in fast food's share of the meals due to the obesity debate and possibly reaching saturation point. The trend towards fast casual dining will suit the concept that The Bistro on Woodlands proposes will take advantage of this decline as an increase in our potential market size and catchment area.

Mintel reports say that the average spend at Pret A Manger is £3.20 compared to a national average of £1.98 per day for lunch highlighting the trend towards premium lines.

For customers, it is reported that lunchtime convenience is the key as well as the fact that food will be good value. This supports the view that location close to popular business areas is vital to attracting high volumes of customers during lunch breaks,

Open to practical development

The buying decision will be made by adults or business policies as they are the economically active and sanction the use of company funds. The figures show that the market is open to practical development as evident by the other restaurants already established in the industry. There are no evident barriers to entry from the customers or incumbents.

The market research activities have highlighted the following groups:
1. 5 – 17 years (teens)
2. 18 – 25 years (teens and young couples)
3. 26 – 49 (including those with young families)
4. 50 + (including those with older families)

This does not mean that the omitted age groups do not eat out. They were not highlighted in our market research.

The market can also be classified as follows:
1. Regular diners (at least once a week)
2. Business diners
3. "If nothing else will do…" (socialites)
4. Reluctant diners
5. Non- diners

Psycho-Demographics

Our market philosophy will be to meet the social aspirations and 'belongingness' by eating out with friends. The customers may also want to dine with us as a treat because they feel they deserve it. The Bistro restaurant will enable the target markets to achieve their self-esteem and status needs. The targeting of businesses will also benefit employee and client relations.

This will be possible as established research and evidence available has shown that the individuals will strive to join a social group that is more reflective of their perceived or aspirational social status.

Customer benefits and Problems solved

The restaurant market in Woodlands area is limited and there are no Bistro restaurants in the locality. The market is characterised by having a few restaurants that serve the community.

One characteristic of the area is the dominance of the Italian and Curry restaurants.

The presence of Sauchiehall Street and other night leisure activities leads to the high level of night activity. There are major night clubs or theatres in the area leading to the residents having to travel to the area from boroughs and the west end for entertainment and eating out. This may be an advantage for those residents that do want to use night busses and taxi fares.

This illustrates the need in Woodlands for an entertainment experience that is pleasurable and brings the community and businesses together in a comfortable and pleasant environment.

We will meet and facilitate for the residents to gather in their social groups and express their need for affection, receiving and giving. This is true of the need for everyone to be appreciated and involved.

The choice of a restaurant eating out experience is affected by four main factors, from the research:
1. Group composition
2. Mental and physical energy
3. location
4. Deals and events

Group composition

The market research has highlighted that the captive audience is more likely to engage in an eating out experience with friends and family. The French Bistro restaurant business concept is more associated with a romantic meal of reasonable quality. This means that the group spend will be much higher and the size of the restaurant will facilitate for the more intimate of meals and a cosy atmosphere between friends.

Mental and physical energy

Some respondents are highly motivated to experience eating out and encourage friends to join them. However, the research also highlighted that some may be tired after work and reserve going out till the end of the week. This is consistent with the findings that Saturday is the busiest day of the week for restaurants and entertainment places. However, the type of restaurant will not be too taxing on the customers and we will not be playing loud music that one would not like to hear at the end of a busy day.

Location

As with restaurants, location is vital. The restaurant is on the same road as the Italian restaurants and other public houses. The location is close to a busy junction between the M8 and Woodlands road. There is also ample car parking. The location is also close to the popular Woodlands Park. The restaurant location is also close to the marriage suites and the University of Glasgow's St. Andrews buildings.

A few yards from the location there is also a bus stop served by the number 118 and 44 buses, among others, to and from the city centre. The location is also within walking distance of the SPT subway stations of St. Georges and Charing Cross.

The area is also serviced by hair dressers and barber shop, in addition to the other local stores including off licences, accountants and estate agents. This will provide a good opportunity to market the restaurant and provide exposure.

The restaurant is also located in an area of low local unemployment. The majority of local residents work in the west end or other parts of the city. This means that the customers have to travel for work and entertainment. The local residents are not currently served by quality eateries. The majority of food establishments are high volume low quality exotic take away.

Deals and events

The restaurant will mostly focus on the evening diner. The main offer will be the 'Gentleman's' offer. This is a package designed to treat, please and delight the customers. It is an ideal tool to maximise the location and psycho-demographics of the intended customers. The package is divided into two and this is designed to maximise the exposure of the deal and attract customers.

This flagship offer is designed to attract customers as a Unique Selling Proposition that features the core products and secondary products in the form of flowers and chocolates plus exclusive menu items. The supplementary products will have the effect of differentiating the core product from competitors and create a competitive advantage.

The supplementary services will also enhance the appeal of the core product. This will provide the options of either purchasing the core product on its own, or with the supplements.

There is also a programme to associate with Hair dressers and Barber shops in the locality. This will involve offer the customers of the local hair dressers a 10% discount on their meal when they get a haircut.

We will also offer 10% off for local emergency services from the Police, NHS and Fire brigade. This is designed to generate sales through increase local rapport and generating word of mouth advertising.

The idea of charging a corkage fee will also prove to be attractive for customers especially seeing as the café has no liquor license. The corkage fee will be £3 for single diners and £4 for couples.

There are also preliminary plans to offer a lunch time menu and take away facility when the service is up and running. This is designed, once again, to add to the core dining market.

The service in customers terms – The Bistro on woodlands road.

> **Features**

A menu featuring many items and split distinctly into three. A Breakfast menu, a Lunch menu and a Diner menu. Each menu will have traditional and modern dishes that are of a bistro style.

Benefits
Our customers will have a large choice of meals and are able to satisfy their individual tastes and circumstances.

Proofs
By only serving Authentic Bistro meals from a set menu, we will ensure that the customers are able to choose what they want and anticipate their meal. We will also offer a selection of fish and vegetarian dishes that are traditionally high in flavour and simple in appeal and preparation.

> **Features**

Table reservations and service bookings available.

Benefits
The customers will be able to reserve their tables and also order the 'Gentleman's' service in advance to ensure availability. This will avoid the disappointment of having to wait while other customers have their meals. The booking system will also allow for us to manage the demand and stock levels. The restaurant will have limited covers and the size will mean that there will be a maximum number of tables available. The booking system will also act as a fair way of allocating the service and avoid customers fighting for the limited seating.

Proof

There will be a reservation system that will feature all the tables and times for staff to record reservations and bookings for the 'Gentleman's' service.

> **Features**

A fixed menu displaying all the dishes and services available in the restaurant window. We will also have a website showing the menu and services available. This is to be introduced at a later stage.

Benefits

This will allow the customers to be able to choose their meals before coming to the restaurant. It will also make it easier for customers to make their decisions when it comes to choosing their meal.

Proof

The menu will be displayed in the window of the restaurant and will be available to take away. A website will also be created to allow customers to view the menu and also act as a contact point. This will later be tied in with the online reservation system.

> **Features**

A quick service restaurant model.

Benefits

The quick service of food will allow for customers to get their meals hot and within a reasonable time. The customers will be able to get their main meals moments after the starter. The customers will be able to order their food, eat and engage in other activities that they may have planned for the night.

Proofs

As the food will be *mise en place*, or fully prepared, the service will be quick as the food preparation time is reduced.

> **Features**

'Bring your own wine'.

Benefits

This allows the customers to bring their own chosen bottle of wine to accompany their meal. This makes it cheaper for them as they will only pay a £3.00 corkage fee for singles and £4 for couples.

The customers will also be able to view our menu and other drinks so that they are informed of our service should they want to return for a night out.

Proofs

The offer will be advertised on the menu and included in all the communications of the restaurant.

Service creation

There are a number of factors that come together to create the service and deliver it to the customers. The relationship between these factors and how they combine is best illustrated by means of a diagram:

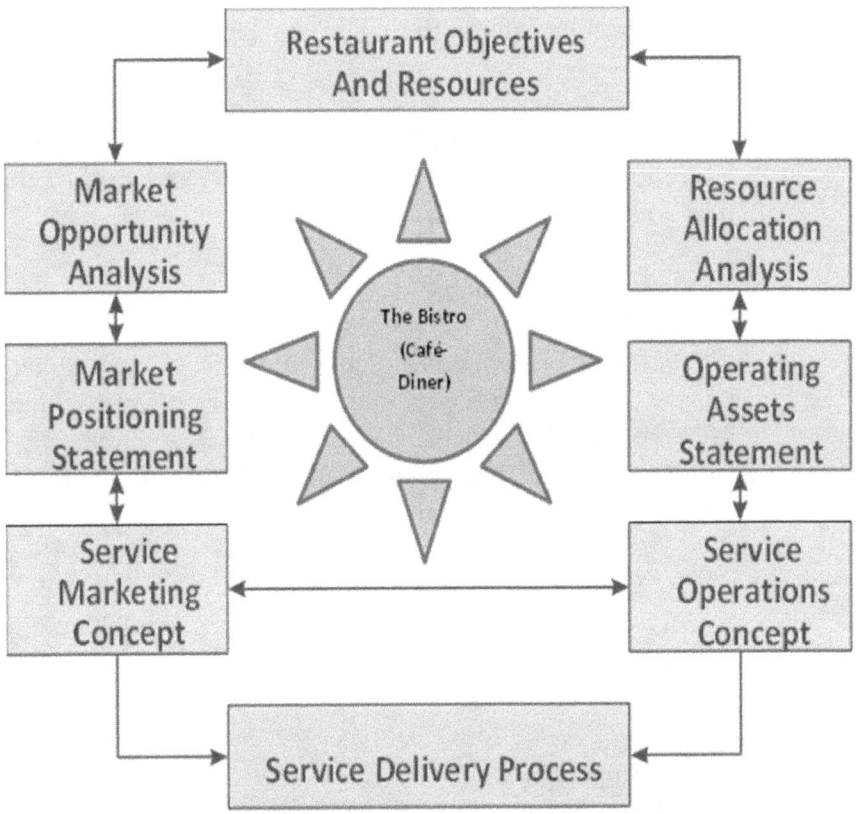

Figure 2 Service Delivery Model

Innovators (First customers)

Our principle customers will be those we have classed as the regular dinners. These diners already exist as evident by the market incumbents. We will aim to attract these diners by advertising and marketing through hair Salons among other avenues. The business concept means that these diners are likely to be 20 years and above living in the local area and with a regular income.

The following describes the factors that are important in the customers' decision to buy or not to buy our service, how much they should buy and how frequently:

Product considerations
- Price-

We will be reflective of the clientele we are attracting. The business model and the menu plus services offered will allow us to offer competitive prices. We will also be purchasing the food stuffs part made and ready-made allow us to benefit from the economies of scale that are associated with large manufacturers.

- Quality –

As our food will be outsourced for a reputable supplier who use economies of scale and scope to produce food of a constant high quality and taste.

- Appearance-

The premises will be kept clean and tidy with the décor reflecting the type of food and service that is associated with the business model. The food will also be presented with flair and care to reflect the origins of this type of restaurant.

The Sales plan

The service will be sold on within the restaurant. We will not be engaging salesman or making sales calls. We will be relying on our marketing activities to drive sales and generate revenue.

The meals will be prepared fresh and to order. This will allow us to offer a fast service and monitors sales easily and effectively. The meals will be presented on white plates and cutlery available. This method will allow us to monitor our food costs and reduce capital tied up in stock.

The selling of the service will also be down to the presentation and service style of the staff. All staff will be trained on the menu and the wines available. They will also be tested and trained on customer service and the company marketing and advertising methods.

The marketing activities that are designed to drive local sales by attracting and generating repeat custom from the local residents.

Our pricing is based on the costs associated with purchasing the products from suppliers. We aim to have a pricing policy that will maintain a fair price for our meals while generating sufficient sales to keep operating. There will be a price spread to reflect the target market and the nature of the restaurant and service offered.

Sales plan: Grand opening

The shop front will be fabricated before the opening. This is designed to increase and maintain the visibility of the store. This is also of low cost and has been proven to be highly successful. In addition, The Grand Opening is important as it helps the image of the restaurant and the perceptions of customers of the restaurant.

The will also be an opening night event where we will invite local business, council officials, local press and local groups. As we are a start-up, we will ask all those that wish to attend to make a contribution of £5 to cover a buffet starter, main course and wine.

Sales Plan: Point of Purchase (P.O.P)

We will use leaflets placed by the door and on table tops to explain the services available, including catering and breakfast options. We will also have takeaway menus for customers to take away. The nature of the business is such that there is no material that can be purchased at the till. This is different to restaurants like Nandos that have a brand in their sauces which they are able to sell to customers.

Sales Plan: Direct mail piece and press campaign

We will use a leaflet that will highlight the opening of the restaurant and the menu that is on offer. This will be included in the local papers as a leaflet so as to target the local residents. The aim of this campaign will be to make it in conjunction with a press release in order to gain the maximum exposure and possible sales.

Sales Plan: Local store marketing

We aim to present the local hairdressers and barbers with an offer of 10% of for their customers when they have a hair-do and dine with us. This is designed to create a relationship with the owners and increase the sales avenues for our restaurant. We will also aim to present a 'free' meal for one nominated council employee every month. This will be designed and marketed as an employee reward scheme that will generate interest and exposure within the local services.

We also aim to offer a similar scheme to the five florists within the target market area. This will help us reach our target market and get on their restaurant radar for eating out recommendations.

Sales Plan: 'Bring your own wine Monday night'

On Mondays' we will charge £3 for customers to bring their own chosen wines and beverages. This allows the customers to 'save' on the wine while enjoying a quality meal.

The Product Plan

Within the restaurant industry, the service often becomes the product. We aim to create a strong brand by linking the service closely with the food. The product may be the food, which is tangible, but the service will also form a large part of the business concept. We aim to serve dishes prepared to order for diner, quick service breakfasts and lunches plus a selection of beverages.

The nature of the kitchen/cooking area is such that the customers will be able to see the cooking taking place. It would be therefore important to have the quality of the food high. This means the meals will be made with fresh ingredients, theatre style.

The menu is light on traditional French sauces which are rich in flavour. It is more soft and light to address the current healthy eating trends. The majority of the foodstuffs are grilled to order and some are marinated using fresh ingredients to boost the build-up of 'good bacteria' and retain vitamins.

It is not enough to prepare the food and then leave it at that. The model is designed to offer a continued marketing service even in the restaurant. This will be achieved through items such as staff training and customer service to clients.

The breakfast menu will feature traditional items such as a Scottish cooked breakfast and include higher margin items such as eggs Benedict and soufflé omelettes. The lunch menu will feature the traditional salads, sandwiches and Panini made or tossed fresh to order.

This will be a great service as we will offer a fresh green salad and a selection of dressings. This would suit the lunch market as well as the diner market.

Unique Selling Proposition (USP)

We aim to be service orientated and deliver quality experiences for our diners. We are going to have a sustained marketing campaign that is designed to engage potential and current diners outside the restaurant. We will target them through associated industries such as Hair dressers and florists. These campaigns are designed to generate sales and increase foot-flow into our restaurant.

We also have a unique open-plan kitchen that allows us to offer the popular theatre style cooking. This will make the destination an elegant and exciting venue to dine for breakfast, lunch or dinner.

We will also have a mix of fresh ingredients to garnish our food to create an exciting presentation. Not all ingredients will be cooked and there is a choice of freshly dressed salad and other bistro style fresh food, never frozen.

The current stage of development

At present, a suitable location has been found in the right location for the business. There will need to be some building work done to make sure that the restaurant functions properly. These are minor works that are largely cosmetic and will take a maximum of 7 days.

The business concept and plans are complete and await financing.

The food and drink will be ordered at the last minute as they may be delivered the following day. This will allow us to have few funds tied up in stock and ensure that we have fresh ingredients all the time.

Window of opportunity

The opportunity is not perpetual as the idea property is still on the market and may be acquired by someone else. It is therefore of paramount importance that the site be secured immediately. There is no available substitutable site in the market, by location alone or even size.

Capital, Labour, Material Proportions

The initial stages of the business model are capital intensive. This is because of the purchases and converting the premises into the desired use. A majority of the start-up costs are for fixed and operating assets with a vital proportion going to marketing and sales generating activities.

Labour

The business model is designed to use part time labour. This reduces the commitment to staff. The nature of the model means that no chef is required and therefore, the costs will be considerably lower. Two members of staff are needed as a bare operational minimum. This is due to the size of the outlet, anticipated demand and reduction in costs.

Material

In this instance, the food will be purchased on a rolling basis. The level of sales will determine the amount of material ordered. These vital variable costs will be monitored constantly. This will not be difficult as there are few menu lines. The use of cost control measures and systems will also ensure that sufficient stock is available for service.

Local authority approvals

The premises benefit from class 3, (café) consent for the ground floor with toilets and storage available down stairs.

The premises will be available to the local environmental health department for inspection although no licences are needed at this time.

Potential liabilities

As a food serving establishment to members of the public, there is need for public liability insurance. There will also be a liability to staff, as an employer. A comprehensive insurance cover will be sought, tailored for cafés and restaurants.

Of importance is the recording and monitoring of food sauces, temperature and condition. These will be monitored starting with the order specifications, goods receiving, recording and storage. In addition, preparation methods and conditions will also be recorded for any potential future reference.

Insurance

There will be the mandatory Public Liability Insurance and Employer's Liability Insurance. There are insurance packages that are available and will cost £600.00 per year that are comprehensive to the restaurant industry. The insurance will also include a business continuity element to cover any disruptions

Resource Plan

The business is that of a restaurant. We will serve prepared to order bistro dishes in an authentic theatre kitchen. The food will consist of a selection of dishes grilled and prepared to order. The preparation method requires quick processes to produce healthy, full flavour meals.

Breakdown of inventory	The Bistro (Café/Diner)		
Restaurant Equipment inventory	Quantity	Cost	Value
Fridge with Digital Temperature			
Cooking Pots			
Sauce pans			
Colour coded chopping boards			
Kitchen knives			
Plates			
Bowls			
Server ware			
Cafetière			
Cutlery			
Table top Menu covers			
Window menu display			
Glassware			
Dishwasher			
Hygiene Fly Trap			
Plastic cutlery tray			
Kitchen Grill			
Stainless steel wall table			
Tables			
chairs			
Microwave oven			
Gass Hob			

Figure 3 Restaurant Equipment Inventory

A complete inventory list including quantities and cost price is included in the Appendix.

Stock levels:

The initial stock levels are to be determined by the meals and beverages that we will offer. We will order the minimum number of stock at the launch. This is in order to avoid having a large stock inventory where some meals may be easy to waste. The numbers are made up of the minimum order cases of the suppliers and to our purchasing specifications. Effective monitoring of this will highlight the popular meals and where we should push the high margin meals to customers.

Regular stock take and daily sales checks will highlight what needs to be ordered for next day delivery. This will allow us to not only measure daily stock levels, but also to provide vital information towards the financial health of the business and is part of the operations plans. The result is reduced funds tied up stock

The stock will be obtained from local suppliers including, **[PROPRIETARY INFORMATION REMOVED]**. They are the largest suppliers and therefore, offer the security of stock availability and quality.

Staff will be recruited from the local area with an advert placed at the local job-centre for free. This will be highly effective as the level of competence required in staff is best suited to this form of local advertising. Our aim is to also get involved with the Glasgow metropolitan college's catering department for staff.

For the inventory, we will be unable to lease any equipment the result being outright purchase. This is to do with the remaining items needed to start and the purchases will be on going, subject to operations review.

We will also have to pay cash for the ingredients and supplies. This is because new restaurants are unable to raise lines of credit with suppliers. The benefit of this is that we will also be able to monitor more closely the funds appreciate cost saving schemes.

All staff will be on part time contracts on a temporary basis for a probation period of three months. A performance and business review will then highlight whether a permanent contract be granted or not. Staff administration systems will also be in place prior to opening.

We will have a next day delivery lead time. This is standard in catering and the suppliers achieve this at all times. This means that we will be able to order stock at the end of business and have it ready for the next trading day in time for opening.

Competition

Direct competitors in close proximity on woodlands road:

1. Subway
2. Grassroots organic food hall
3. Beanscene coffee house
4. A Slice Above
5. Big Bites café
6. The Bento bar (pub and restaurant)
7. Balti club (take away)
8. Sainsbury's local
9. Crepe a croissant
10. Café la Padella – Italian restaurant and organic food
11. The Arlington pub
12. Torna Sorrento Italian restaurant
13. The Halt pub
14. Chillies takeaway.
15. The Primary pub

Pricing

Our menu prices will vary to include items in different price ranges. For breakfast, traditional items such as roll and sausage will be cheap at 80p. This is very cheap on our part as our customers can dine and be serviced for such cheap meals. The price range that we have chosen is also the range offered by the nearby restaurants. We will also offer more indulging items such as eggs Benedict and eggs St. Charles with a higher price range.

For dinners, we will be relatively cheaper because we offer one price for the complete meal as opposed to the Chinese and Indian restaurants that have a separate price for the main dish sauce and an additional charge for the rice and/or noodles. This means that the restaurants ultimately have higher total revenue but their meals will be more expensive compared to our one price for a dish pricing policy. For example, steak frites will come with a garden side salad and fish dishes with garlic French beans.

To summarise, the pricing policy will be tiered as follows:
- Matching competitors prices
- Calculating prices from costs and cost percentages
- Adding my desired contribution margins to portion costs.

Competitor's reactions

We have not built in a fall-back position as the market is unable to cut prices. The restaurants and eating places in the area are of different concepts and styles. Our decision not to focus on alcohol, despite the profit, means that we will not compete on price for drinks. There are already two Italian restaurants close by and these open late and are open till late. We are in a different market as we will open at 7am and close at 8pm when most restaurants are expecting their busy trade. The Cafés are open from 0730 till 1500 while the restaurants open later and serve till 2300.

Research has shown that restaurants are busiest in the evening between 1830hrs and 2130 with the busiest time being 2000, for bookings.

We will focus on quality produce and meals as this is more important than competing on price. Price competition will also affect the bistro image and concept central to the restaurant.

By lowering their prices, the restaurants will then fall into this inferior market bracket associated with low quality, unhygienic ingredients and premises.

Our prices will reflect the size of the café as customers will not expect to spend £15 on a steak at such an eatery. Our pricing policy is based on the cost of the ingredients as based on our cost sheets and mark up of at least 75%. Steak dishes and mussels will be our signature dishes and will therefore be priced differently.

This makes us cheaper than 'tablecloth' restaurants and the majority of local eateries. There is no doubt that pizzas have a greater mark-up but fail to add value through service delivery and aesthetic appeal necessary for marketing and PR.

This makes our pricing policy relatively cheap compared to other restaurant main meals. We also have a selection of quality enhancing presentations such as adding fresh rocket after cooking the meals for more added-value. Market research has shown that using fresh ingredients for presentations also enhances the value and the amount customers are willing to pay for fresh products.

As with French food, presentation is important as it conveys care and love of food as opposed to the rustic and 'thrown' together approach of Italian food.

SWOT Analysis

Competitors' Strengths and Weaknesses.
The competitors are already established within the local market. This gives them an advantage as the incumbents. The geographical market is well served as the competitors are spread throughout the borough in and around the west end.

The direct competitor is the Italian pizza and pasta restaurants on Woodlands road. It is strong in that is offers customers a choice of pastas and asks them to choose their favourite sauce. Café La Padella also focuses on organic food principles as its unique selling proposition.

There is also Chilli's down the road which offers tandoori cooking and take away pizza.

The major disadvantage is that the restaurant is mostly a take-away venue with four metal tables where the customers can sit while they wait for their food. This does not classify the outlet as a restaurant.

It will be easy to take market share from this incumbent as we will offer clients an opportunity to have their meals within the restaurant or to take away. This is a highly effective strategy that is already used by other restaurateurs.

Our competitive edge is the menu, the environment and service delivery model. We have a marketing campaign that includes items our competitors will not offer. We will also be able to produce our food fast and fresh to meet the customer demands quickly, effectively and customer friendly.

Using set menu's for breakfast and dinner service will ensure that we reduce waste and are able to offer items as 'extras' for PR and marketing purpose to add to the other trade building activities.

Opportunities

The competition is focused on serving different market segments to those that we intend to target. Café La Padella is targeted at family diners as outlined by their menu design and the offers that they have. The Chilli's take away restaurant targets the takeaway market and offers no dining facilities.

We aim to serve the business diners as our core target market. This is illustrated by our emphasis on service, environment and consistent high quality food. Our location close to the M8 allows us to offer a dinning service as our customers are able to drive and park their vehicle while they dine with us. In the restaurant trade, business dinning is singled out as a more lucrative market for restaurants as diners often do not worry about the cost.

As we do not have a liquor license, the corkage concept will prove to be highly attractive as there is a major off license close by. We will seek to have our menu available for viewing in the off license so customers can choose their drinks to suit the menu.

Threats

The premises are still available on the open market. There is a risk that they may be taken off the market and occupied by someone else. We will not be able to start-up at the preferred location, if this is the case.

Not having an alcohol license means that we not be able to offset the revenues against food sales. However, the corkage fee means customers have a greater choice and are able to choose the drinks they want. This will further enhance out appeal as a destination venue and add to our PR activities.

Competitor's reactions
We have built in a fall-back position although the market is unable to cut prices. There are many 'Pizza fast food restaurants' such as Chilli's that offer customers cheap pizza for £3 to £5. These are cheap pizzas where the customers have to choose between two and four toppings. The cheese used is also of inferior quality and the resulting product is also of inferior quality.

By lowering their prices, the pizza houses will then fall into this inferior market bracket associated with low quality, unhygienic ingredients and premises.

Our emphasis is not on cheap food or fine dining but offering the Bistro experience in an environment that appeals to the needs of our target market. As such, we will not charge excessively high prices for our food.

Our meals are made in the traditional sizes and constitute a full main course. This makes our pricing policy relatively cheap compare to other restaurant main meals. We also have a selection of quality enhancing presentations such as adding fresh parsley after cooking the dishes for more added value. Our side orders are also of extremely high quality in keeping with the continental Bistros. Market research has shown that using fresh ingredients for presentations also enhances the value and the amount customers are willing to pay for fresh products.

Competitive Advantage

We will be offering a dining experience not currently available within the local market. The geographical layout of the area warrants for a deviation from focusing on foot flow alone. We will be marketing our Unique selling Propositions and engaging in cross selling through local small businesses.

Our service creation model has allowed us to focus on the customers. We will aim to serve our clients and treat them with the greatest of customer care rather than relying on our food to sell for us. This brings about the billion dollar question, 'how many people can make a better beef burger than McDonalds?. The lunch and evening menu is focused and we will change it every four months in keeping with the seasons and market prices.

We have the intention of creating a brand by distinguishing our restaurant through marketing, sales activities and focus on customer care. We will listen to our customers by constantly asking them if they like their meal and if they have any comments.

The plan is to have the restaurant as aesthetically pleasing as possible while focussing on the desired image and restaurant concept. We will be an evening dining restaurant with afternoon sales, excellent systems and customer care.

The location is also excellent for driving customers as it is close to the M8 and Great Western Road.

The area is also populated by other restaurants', which makes it ideal as there is evidence of an existing market.

Marketing Strategy

The market research has indicated that the average independent restaurant spends £1,200.00 per campaign and mostly in local newspapers that do reviews and have listing pages for eating out places to visit. The advertising is also said to tend to be seasonal, targeting the markets for eating out at festive seasons, such as Christmas or Easter, and also with promotions around Mother's day or Valentine's Day. It is also said that Advertorial features might also be available on a seasonal basis, coupling with editorial recommendations, that is, public relations, rather than media advertising.

It is also said that direct marketing is an important promotional tool for many local restaurants. In particular, door-to-door drops of menus or flyers are useful for restaurants that offer both eat-in and takeaway, with home delivery an option.

Current market

The local market is characterised by pubs and Italian, Indian and fast food restaurants. There are places that serve pizza and Tandoori but there is no provision for dining. The products on offer are also aimed at the fast food market. There is a restaurant currently serving quality fresh pizza within a dining environment and its main focus is also organic food.

The breakfast market is currently served by two eateries at the top of Woodlands road for hot food. The local grocers also sell sandwiches and takeaway drinks.

Benefits of our service

We will serve fresh breakfasts and a range of main meals to the evening adult dining market. Our environment will be stimulating and presenting an aesthetic environment for quality bistro dining. We also aim to introduce a delivery service specific to businesses in the local area.

Customer needs we will fill

There are no quality dining restaurants serving site down breakfasts and Bistro dishes in the Woodlands area. The market is littered with fast food and 'Pizza and kebab' restaurants.

We will offer an alternative, differentiate, and become one of the few quality restaurants in the area. This niche will allow us to generate enough customers to continue to offer our customers value for money.

In order to optimise the number of customers, I have taken into account the factors that affect potential customer's selection of restaurants:

1. Location issues will not allow us to focus on volume or post 2000hrs dining market.
2. Menu item differentiation, that is, signature dishes.
3. Price acceptability for our type of eatery and menu.
4. Décor, which will reflect The Bistro on Woodlands concept.
5. Portion sizes to reduce waste and food costs.
6. Quality of dishes.
7. Menu diversity.

Marketing and Advertising objectives

We aim to raise awareness of our market presence and products and services offered. We aim to be included when our target market is considering making their buying decisions to eat in a restaurant or treat themselves or a loved one. We aim to be included when our target market is considering treating themselves or spending time satisfying their sociological and emotional needs through eating out.

The main areas of profitability are the menu design and the sales techniques used by staff. For marketing and advertising, the menu will be constructed taking into consideration its layout, variety (of items and preparation techniques), item arrangement and location on the menu, descriptive language plus the kitchen personnel and equipment.

The staff will also be taught the selling techniques, **[PROPRIETARY INFORMATION REMOVED]**, to use in The Bistro and also be briefed about every item on the menu including the ingredients and preparation methods.

Additional costs of achieving marketing and advertising objectives

A fixed cost figure of £300 per month will aimed for. In total, this budgeted figure is three times the amount said to be average of independent restaurants. We will aim for 'below the line' advertising. This is consistent with new businesses and is known to be more effective for our target market. The budget will 'kick-in' when we have established trade level able to sustain it. At present, the whole business will be a marketing centre with emphasis on service, quality and cleanliness.

We will use traditional methods for restaurants that include local newspaper advertising and the use of flyers.

Method

The restaurant should be available at the start of the consumer purchase decision path. When our target market is evaluating eating out, they will consider the type of environment and service they wish to experience. We wish to be present at this stage. This normally takes place when the target markets are treating themselves, for example, to a haircut. We will achieve this through the planned promotions through the local hair dressers. We will offer 10% to the hair salons or barbers customers. We will also have a 10% off programme for local florist customers.

This method will cost us £1 in every £10 and is consistent with the traditional method of spending 10% of the previous year's sales. This method results in high spending after a good year and so-on. As a start-up, our method is the best as it allows us to offer the advertising spend along with sales. The overall effect is that for 10% of marketing we get 90%, upfront. It will also be extremely effective to monitor the effectiveness of this method.

It is also an easy system to administer and is a highly effective above the line marketing and advertising method.

The decision is also made in other areas and times. An example is at the end of the working day after a good or bad days work. Having a captive audience at this stage is difficult. We will however, have a sustained marketing plan that will allow for our target market to be constantly informed of our services. This sustained activity will allow for our customers to evaluate us given the experiences they seek having encountered us through above the line advertising and marketing.

The message we will convey through literature and other promotions is that we will offer a dining environment of quality food and service. When our target market wishes to treat themselves to quality ingredients, excellent service and pleasant experiences they will be aware of us. We will highlight our Bistro and breakfast themes that feature free range eggs, fresh rocket and other dishes individually made to order with the freshest ingredients.

We will also have friendly employees that undergo regular training and appraisals to maintain customer service standards to the desired high level. This is part of the administration plan and will be monitored by the employee development files. Training will also include restaurant sales training to enable staff to sell dishes to customers at the table. The chosen techniques know to management and to be used are **[PROPRIETARY INFORMATION REMOVED]**

Of great importance will be the ability of service personnel to describe the dishes to customers and 'sell' them at the table when the plate arrives just as the food is about to be placed into the mouth. This is part of the after sales care which will increase the level of enjoyment of the dish and the likelihood of repeat service.

Our complaints handling will also be used as a marketing and advertising initiative. We will offer replacement meals that will have resolved the customer's complaints to show that we have listened and are able to respond to requests. As part of the PR initiative, we may occasionally offer free samples of our dishes.

The focus will be on trying to create a strong peer-to-peer marketing campaign by creating a service that generates excellent experiences for our customers. By meeting, and continually exceeding their expectations with regard to emotions and feelings we will be associated with pleasant experiences that will generate conversations. This advertising is crucial and priceless.

The décor will also be of high quality as the restaurant will be new and many of the materials will be aesthetically pleasing and delightful to the eye. There will be simple décor with quality tables and chairs, minimal artwork and ambient lighting. The lighting is also known as mood lighting.

In conclusion, customers should buy from us because we – the restaurant- are different. We will offer a niche service, not obtrusive, focused on customer care with emphasis on goodwill and pleasant behaviour, especially mannerisms.

Customers should buy from us because it – the food – is different. We will have a selection of main meals that will be constant in high quality and consistent. We will also be offering fresh dishes made to order with the freshest ingredients. The dishes include the signature steak frites and salads.

Of great importance will be the preparation methods and variety of ingredients used for the menu.

We have a combination of presentation styles and techniques that will differentiate the dishes. We will use fresh basil and presentations. We will not smother all our meals in cheap genetically modified cheese and leave customers guessing what is underneath when the cheese crust slides off with one dreaded bite, and does not separate.

Media

Yellow pages, Thompson's and BT

We will use the yellow pages to place a free advert that is offered to all businesses. This is because is said that directory listings are important for consumers to be able to find a local restaurant/café or at least to track down its telephone number to make a booking.

There will also be an editorial that will be sent to the local guardian free paper. This is included in the appendix.

There is a price list included. This is also the menu and will be available to take away by customers.

There is a plan to create a discount list that features 'the blue lights'. This will be a service that will be offered to members of the emergency services. The Fire brigade, police and ambulance staff will get a 10% discount with their meals. This will be done by sending a letter to the offices/bases of the services informing them of the discount.

There is also a plan to sponsor a media competition by offering the winner a free meal if they win and are over 18. This will allow for us to get some above the line advertising. A description of what is available will be offered to entice entrance to the competition offering a free quality meal.

In order to get our target market, we will have to leaflet the local area through either inserts or loose leaflets. This is best done at the local train stations and may be cheap and highly effective for rush hours

Marketing and Advertising competitive difference

We will be the only restaurant to offer Local Area Businesses Marketing through Hair Salons and barbers. This is unlike our competitors.

We will also offer a blue lights discount which is the first of its kind in the local restaurant area.

We will also engage in competitions giveaways which are not currently practised by the incumbents.

Future markets

There is a strong possibility for a delivery service. This will allow us to serve within the café and also deliver to customers. There will be an opportunity to spread the fixed assets over other services such as a lunch opening and catering service to the local area and Businesses.

Mintel reports that 33% of people will tend to eat the same type of food for lunch and 23% will buy from the same place each day. This may be for a lack of available outlets to purchase from and necessitate repetition. Developing a client base will probably insure future business and starting this Bistro will offer alternatives that were previously unavailable.

Industry and market watch

There will be a subscription to the Restaurant magazine and catering and hotelier magazines. This will allow us to be in touch with the restaurant market. We will also participate in the Glasgow business of the year awards and join the local small business forum. Membership of the Glasgow chamber of commerce is also planned at an estimated cost of £200 for the first year.

Mintel reports that customers are willing to spend £1.98 per day or £5 per five day working week on lunch time meals. It also says that cost is not the most important factor when selecting lunch. Taste health and convenience are said to be more important criteria although customers are still looking for value-for-money and product quality.

For lunch service, it is said that 20-24 year olds in the south regularly skip lunch most likely due to being more time pressured, an always in a rush lifestyle. However, this does not include Londoners.

It is also said that consumers are taking the longest lunch in a decade at an average of 36minutes and there is a preference to snack rather than have a full meal.

Place and distribution

The Bistro restaurant concept requires premises with a dining area of at least 300 sq.ft and a connected ancillary area of at least 90sq. ft. these would be the minimum ground floor plans. There are no intentions to acquire premises with an upstairs area as this may not comply with Health and Safety. It also splits the dining area and will fail to meet the criteria needed to create the right atmosphere for the restaurant.

The restaurant may be located in quieter areas of the town as this fits in with the target market who will not want to associate with the binge drinking culture of high street pubs and clubs.

The chosen location, 146 Woodlands road, is close to a free parking space and a major intersection. The location is also within walking distance of St. Georges and Charing Cross stations of the SPT services. There is also a bus stop a few yards away for the 118 and 44 buses and a few more buses at the nearby busy junction.

Woodlands road is also close to the Great Western road which is a major access route for the city centre.

Location type advantages

This location offers a competitive advantage in that the area suits the target market. it is calm with a medium foot flow and is very close to car parking area. It is also close to Kelvingrove Park and the University of Glasgow's St. Andrews building. The area is also near other restaurants and leisure activities such as the pool house and mosque.

The premises create the desired atmosphere and the size allows us to charge less for our quality food making us more competitive.

The premises already have a café licence.

Premises

The premises are located at 146 Woodlands road. It has been said by the landlords that the café has seating for 36 and has been recently refurbished to a high standards to produce hot food.

The rent is estimated at £250 per week with the rateable value at £5,000.00 and the rates payable, including small business relief at £1,807.00 for 2005/06.

The utilities bill is guesstimated to be low given the size of the premises.

Operating and Control Systems

This is the model that will be used to monitor and control the venture.

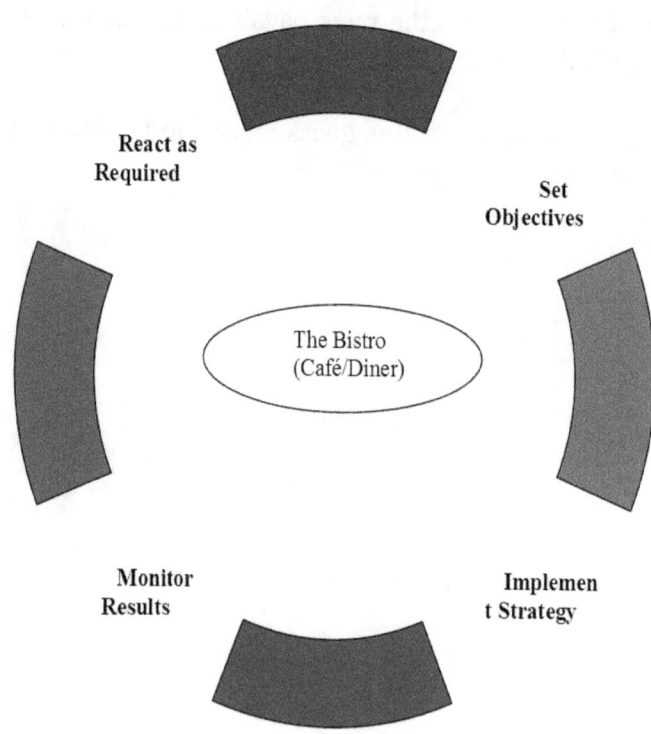

Figure 4 Operating and Control System

FOOD MANUAL

I have created a food manual for The Bistro restaurant concept. This will be used to ensure consistency of quality in the service delivery. The food manual created will also be use full when there is a change of staff.

1. The specifications for the raw ingredients, cook times and temperature for each item and the size of each portion.
2. Preparation procedures
3. Holding times and temperatures.
4. Procedures for handling surplus product.
5. Food storage procedures
6. Food safety procedures
7. Food cost for each portion and suggested price
8. A nutritional analysis of each menu item or dish.

Employee Theft

There are three main types of employee theft that will be mentioned in The Bistro concept:
1. under-ringing of sales and tearing up of food tickets
2. food theft or taking home supplies
3. Leaving and coming in at a later time to clock out.

The operations manual contains details of how to detect employee theft through:
- signals from personal behaviour
- signals from employee behaviour
  - signals from customers and outsiders

Internal security measures

These are some of the measures to be used to control employee theft:
1. Provide information on internal security measures
2. Surveillance
3. Inventory checks
4. Information on the likelihood and consequences of being caught stealing.
5. CASH control measures

This information is highly sensitive, it has therefore, not been included in the open business plan of The Bistro.

Selling and sales management

The advertising and marketing activities will be used to drive sales. We will augment this by offering a great service and having a constant message in the local area.

Our sales and marketing controls will seek to monitor the effectiveness of plans. We will monitor the results of various activities such as Local Area Businesses Marketing (LABM). This is a first for a restaurant in the area and will further enhance our reputation and drive sales.

This is an extract from the system that will be used to monitor the sales:

Week Beginning	No. of enquiries received – emial Phone/foot flow	No. of leaflets received/sent	LABM	Blue lights	Cost of weeks activities	Estimate of sales worth of weeks activities

Figure 5 Sales Monitoring System

The information will be entered onto the system from a telephone sheet and receipts. This is a management function and Allen Mbengeranwa will be responsible for this activity.

Employee related systems

There will be files created for each employee. These will include:
1. Contract of employment
2. Pay records and details including PAYE and National Insurance
3. Job description pack and completed application form
4. Interview responses and health questionnaires
5. Training and development plan and records
6. Evaluations and disciplinary

Customers and marketing systems

1. Complaints procedure and reporting
2. Discounts and offers systems that allow for easy monitoring and evaluation.
3. Refunds procedure.

Premises and Assets Administration

There will be an assets register which will include:
1. Equipment type, supplier and purchase costs
2. Warranty details and maintenance records/check
3. Cleaning schedule
4. Insurance details
5. Operating manual and training guide.
6. Copy of lease and physical building items

Legal and insurance issues

This section will include files on:
1. Insurance policy and cover
2. Lease details contract and solicitors affairs
3. Details of any warrantees and liability issues
4. Council affairs such as planning and building control
5. Environmental health correspondence and requirements

Suppliers

This includes:
1. List of products and services
2. Ordering procedure and lead times
3. Any warrantees and liabilities
4. Conditions of sale
5. Price checks and comparisons

This material has been summarised as it is commercially sensitive material.

Financial Administrative policies, procedures and controls

There will be systems for:
1. H M Customs and revenue
   - PAYE and National Insurance
   - VAT records and payments
   - Business tax
2. financial controls
   - Daily and weekly cash reporting
   - Weekly profit and loss reporting
   - Quarterly fixed assets report
   - Monitoring of daily stock and cash
   - Product costs and profitability
   - Monthly balance sheet
   - Stock control

The role of IT in delivering controls

The aim is to use a computer to monitor all the systems. To begin with, in-house systems have been developed in excel and word. However, for greater efficiency and operations integration, the following items will be needed:

1. Internet enabled computer system with windows operating system
2. Sage ONE accounting software
3. Sage Payroll bureau software
4. Restaurant software with reservations, stock control, point of sale
5. Scanner
6. Colour printer

It should be noted that some of the activities outlined above will be conducted using the created excel programmes and worksheets that I have created until the systems are available. The commercial systems will be more advanced and linked enabling greater analysis and monitoring of the business model.

Administration infrastructure

The following will be necessary to maintain and operate the control systems:
1. Office desk and chair
2. Large secure filling unit
3. Notice board

Contingency Plans

Sales projections

The sales are based on the lower end of the market research assumptions. There is capacity to cater for an increase in sales of 100%. In the event that this does happen, the booking system will be adhered to as a queuing system.

If the sales are less than expected, there will be a drive to increase advertising and marketing. We will speed up the process of developing the business to increase the revenue streams and thus total revenue. The facilities for take away and delivery will be implemented and improved and the respective business plans created. There are intentions to present a business plan for these additional revenue streams 6 months after opening.

At the projected level of sales, there is a fall-back position as the waste will be lower because some of the menu items are frozen, dry goods or ordered fresh the previous day for next day delivery. This is proven to reduce waste while maintaining the quality of produce used. This method also ensures that there are minimum funds tied up in working capital.

There are plans to offer a 'chefs special of the day' during lunch hours and diner. This will be used to drive sales and increase awareness of the restaurant generating 'peer-to-peer' marketing that may lead to an increase in evening diners. The budget for this will come under the PR activities.

The business may develop to offer catering to business and households to provide canapés and snacks. This will be pushed with a business plan and implemented to ease the pressure on the restaurant.

The business model is such that there staff hours of work can be cut. This will be done if the sales prove to be less than anticipated while the marketing and advertising is highlighted. For this, industry labour count techniques will be used given the level of sales.

Supply deficiencies

There are a number of suppliers who will offer the same products as our chosen suppliers. We will contact another company for the menu items. This will not be difficult as we will be using bidding sheets and **[PROPRIETARY INFORMATION REMOVED]**.

We will be able to push the food available that night till the next day's delivery. This will be incorporated into the daily briefings for service staff by management. There are no major problems associated with supply.

Product liability problems arise

As our food will be from established suppliers, we will seek to indemnify ourselves from any liabilities by pursuing suppliers as soon as any issues are identified. All the foodstuff will be sourced from industry accredited and recognised suppliers where every product is traceable. The operating procedures will include goods received and storage instructions and well as recording sheets and labels.

There is also an insurance policy that will cover the usual liabilities associated with restaurants.

Personnel problems

The business model requires low staffing levels and therefore, any issues that arise may be attended to quickly and efficiently. In the event of an employee having to leave, there is capacity for the business to continue operating with one member of staff while recruitment is taking place. It will be explained to customers that there are staff shortages and minor delays may occur.

Capital Expenditure

Equipment required

This list will vary depending on the size of outlet and what is currently available; some items have been omitted for proprietary purposes. The current location also has some of the items listed below.

1.1.1. Commercial fridge with digital temperature displays
1.1.2. Commercial freezer with digital temperature displays
1.1.3. Four ring gas burner and an optional solid top surface
1.1.4. Baine Marie
1.1.5. Salamander grill
1.1.6. Blast Chiller
1.1.7. Cooking equipment
1.1.8. Server ware and table ware

Not all the items listed above will be needed at the start –up.

Start Up Costs

These will depend on the outcome of partnership negotiations for premises and labour costs. However, an ingoing food stock bill of £700.00 is estimated. This is divided into perishable and non-perishable food items. Within this budget, there is also the cost of toiletries and consumables.

The assets cost is estimated at £2,335.36. This includes a main freezer, commercial dishwasher, fly killers and cutlery.

The improvements to fixtures and fittings are estimated at £800.00 and this involves mostly internal paint work and shop front improvements.

The solicitor's fees and marketing costs have been put at £200.00 and £300.00 respectively.

The working capital requirements are put down to £4,000.00 in addition to 'key money' of £2,000.00.

The top-end estimated costs come up to a total of £10,335.36.

The Bistro (Café/Diner) Start-Up Costs

Start-up Costs including both the one-time initial costs needed to open doors and the ongoing costs for the first 90 days.

Start-up Capital Requirements

One-time Start-up Expenses

Start-up Expenses	Amount	Description
Advertising	300	Promotion for opening the business
Starting inventory	700	Amount of inventory required to open
Building construction	500	Amount per contractor Quote
Cash		Amount needed for the cash register/Till
Decorating	300	Estimate based on quote if appropriate
Fixtures and equipment	2335.36	Using actual bids
Insurance	600	Quote from insurance agent
Lease payments	2000	Fees to be paid before opening
Licenses and permits		Check with Local Authorities
Miscellaneous		All other
Professional fees	200	Include accountant, Solicitor, etc.
Remodeling		Use contractor bids
Rent	1000	Fee to be paid before opening
Services		Cleaning, Waste, etc.
Signs		Using contractor bids
Supplies		Office, cleaning, etc. supplies
Unanticipated expenses		Including an amount for the unexpected
Total Start-up Costs	7,935.36	Amount of costs before opening

Figure 6 The Bistro Start-Up Costs

The Bistro (Café/Diner) Start-Up Costs

Start-up Capital Requirements
Repeating Monthly Expenses for 3 months

Expenses	Amount	Description
Advertising	900	
Bank service fees		
Credit card charges		
Delivery fees		
Dues and subscriptions		
Insurance	150	Exclude amount on preceding page
Interest		
Inventory		See **, below
Lease payments		Exclude amount on preceding page
Loan payments		Principal and interest payments
Office expenses	150	
Payroll other than owner	4220	
Payroll taxes		
Professional fees		
Rent	2000	Exclude amount on preceding page
Repairs and maintenance		
Sales tax/VAT		
Supplies	400	
Telephone/Internet	40	
Utilities	150	
Your salary	1500	If applicable for first three months
Other		
Total Repeating Costs	9,510	
Total Start-up Costs	7,935.36	Amount from preceding page
Total Cash Needed	**17,445.36**	

Figure 7 The Bistro Capital Requirement

Staffing Requirements

There will be two members of staff needed to operate the business model. These will be split into shifts and more employees taken on part-time contracts. This is standard practice of the restaurant industry. Ideally, the staff will be French speaking with customer service experience and fast. The work areas will be split into front of house and kitchen support.

Plans are underway to use the local jobcentres on Bath Street and Partick to recruit employees. It is aimed to take advantage of employer incentives in order to reduce the wage bill.

Legal Aspects

Business Status

The status of the business is under review as a partnership with the landlords is sought to reduce the initial bills, particularly rent. This may be in the form of a management contract with the landlords retaining the lease and property ownership in return for a 50/50 profit share.

The record keeping and administration will also be of great detail as this may limit future liability. These activities will also ensure that cost are minimised, profits managed and effectively monitored. The records will range from delivery checking notes and inspection reports to mandatory items such as refrigerator temperature checks and pest control records.

Other Legal Requirements

Health and safety procedures and training. These will be carried out to comply with the councils environmental health departments. We will also involve the council in our pest control and fire procedures.

A folder for all the dishes preparation and storage including cooking temperatures and refrigeration will also be kept for health and liability issues.

Guidelines for food purchasing and supplier accreditation will also be kept and recorded for all perishable items.

Insurance

Building and Contents Insurance.

Comprehensive café insurance. This will include Employer's Liability Insurance and public liability cover.

Financial Information

It would be ideal to grow the business through cash flow. This means that the business will have to grow slower than would be ideal. However, this gives the opportunity to refine the business model and make more accurate assumptions and predictions.

As this is a start-up, the cash flow and profit and loss positions will be monitored more closely as the business is cash heavy with no initial credit terms. The chosen software is able to function at his level plus provide even more detailed analysis.

Financing requirements

The finance required amounts for start-up is £10,335.36. The funding is needed to purchase fixed assets, shop fabrication, start-up and working capital.

The Bistro (Café/Diner)

Financial allocation	Amount
Fixed assets and structural works	£2,335.36
Fixtures and fittings	£800.00
Stock	£700.00
Fees	£200.00
Marketing	£300.00
Key money	£2,000.00
Working capital	£4,000.00
Total	£10,335.36

Figure 8 Financial Requirements

The revenue that will be received will immediately be put towards the working capital. This has the effect of reducing our demands on the funding requirements. It would therefore, be beneficial to have the financing arranged in stages so as to absorb the revenue.

Important assumptions

The assumptions are based on monthly and annual positions.

Important assumptions
The assumptions are based on monthly and annual positions.

%	2005	2006	2007
Tax rate £10-50K	23.75	23.75	23.75
VAT	17.5	17.5	17.5
Interest rates-	11.5%	11.5%	11.5%
National insurance	18	18	18

Figure 9 Financial Assumptions

Pricing Method

Prices will be based on the cost of the ingredients with seasonal variations to reflect the market prices. The aim is to cost every dish and have a minimum of 70% mark up to reflect other items such as gas and cooking oil that are difficult to cost per dish.

The pricing policy will, in summary, be threefold:
- Matching competitors prices
- Calculating prices from Costs and Cost Percentages
- Adding my desired contribution margins to portion costs.

Payment Method

We will accept cash, with safeguards and fraud checks. This will include looking for the watermark on notes and using an electronic note checker. It is planned to introduce chip and pin for credit card purchases. Cheques will not be accepted.

Sales receipts and order pads will also be monitored to reduce the risks associated with revenue collection and staff deception.

Break even Calculation

The Bistro (Café/Diner)	
Break Even Sales	
Some of the material figures used in the break even calculation:	
Rent	£13,000.0
Rates	£1,807.0
Insurance	£600.0
Telephone	£360.0
Total fixed cost	£15,767.0
Selling Price minus Unit Variable Costs	
. : Annual Break Even Sales (Meals)	3,153.4
# Monthly Break Even Sales (Meals)	242.5

Figure 10 Break Even

Gross Profit Margin Calculation

These figures will be monitored on a regular basis to ensure that they will be met. The factors will be varied according to circumstances and trends.

Any profits will accumulate at the gross profit margin rate, 75%. The figures will be affected by:

- Actual level of sales achieved
- Increase/decrease in gross margin
- Increase/decrease in overheads
- There is potential to extract value from the flat, which is not in current use. This will have the effect of reducing the overheads and the actual sales needed for break even

The factors will be varied according to the trend and outcomes from the business.

The management of cash flow and constant monitoring of sales will allow the business model to vary the staff costs in accordance with peak periods and reduce the general staffing levels accordingly.

Sales Forecast

The sales activities have been divided into three revenue streams. These are breakfast service, lunch service and diner service. The sales are estimated at £20.83, £62.50 and £83.33 respectively per day.

Cash flow forecast summary

The Bistro (Café/Diner)

Cash Flow Sheet

Projected Sales	36000
Cash Receipts (Breakfast)	6000
Cash Receipts (Lunch)	18000
Cash Receipts (Diner)	25000
Sales Invoiced	**1800**
Collections from accounts receivable	1000
Total Cash In	**51800**
Cash Disbursements (Cash out)	
Purchases (direct food expenses)	2400
Advertising	1500
Loan Interest	826.8
Insurance (Business Liability)	360
Professional Fees (Accounting & Legal)	200
Rent (Equipment)	0
Rent (Premises) + Rates	14807.04
Telephone and fax	160
Utilities	800
Marketing	200
Wages (Employees & payroll deductions)	26997.96
Loan Payments (capital NOT interest)	2067.24
Office Supplies & Expenses	240
Training	400
Total Cash Out	**50959.04**
Cash Flow Summary	
Opening Balance	840.96
Add: Cash In	51800
Subtract: Cash Out	50959.04
Surplus or (Deficit)	840.96
Closing Cash Balance	**1681.92**

Notes

Wages are based on a 30hr day £5.50p/hr and a 6 day week
National insurance is £2,317per annum
Weekly sales are estimated at £750 i.e 3.75 times the food costs

Figure 11 Cash Flow Forecast Summary

Cash flow forecast assumptions

These are:
- The restaurant will be operational as soon as possible; however, the financial year will run from 06 April to 05 April. This is to coincide with the tax year and group Christmas and summer sales together.
- There are no credit arrangements with suppliers or customers
- The sales have been estimated using the market research evidence. This includes observing the competition in the local area for customer numbers. Although this may not be definitive, it does provide a guide and a yardstick for our sales figures.

There is a pre trading cash-flow statement and a trading statement. The object of the two is to show the movement of money, on an assumption and estimation basis, into and out-from the restaurant.

A restaurant is a cash rich business that has little or no credit facilities. As this is a start-up, there are no assumptions for credit from either suppliers or to customers.

The nature of this business model requires there to be a careful and constant monitoring of the financial position and forecasts. This will be done by using the selected accounting software and the excel programmes and sheets that I have created.

Appendices

The Bistro Breakfast menu

The Bistro (Café/Diner)

Breakfast menu

French toast (regular: deluxe)

Scottish

Farmhouse

Vegetarian

Eggs Benedict

Scrambled eggs on toast/muffin

Beans on toast

Poached egg nestling in ham served on a muffin

Angles on horseback

Soufflé omelette with chunky mushroom sauce

French croissants

Toast and preserves

Swiss Muesli

Cereal

Fresh fruit

Breakfast Panini

Muffin/Bagel and sausage

Muffin/Bagel and bacon

Muffin/Bagel and potato scone

Muffin/Bagel and poached egg

The Bistro Main meals and accompaniments

The Bistro (Café/Diner)

Main menu

Steak frites with shallot butter

Cotelette de Porc Chacuterie / Pork chops with piquant sauce
Le grand Aioli Marseille

Moules a la Bauillabaise/ Mussels with fennel, tomato garlic and saffron

Poulat a la Moutarde de Dijon / Marinated chicken breast in Dijon sauce

Magret de Canard sauce au Poivre / Duck breast with Peppercorns

Salade de Canard Fume / Smoked duck salad

Sole Meuniere

Crevette a l'ail / Garlic prawns

Ratatouille

Sides

Hariocots vets a l'ail/ French beans with garlic

Carottes a crème aux herbes / Carrots with cream and herbs

Gratin Dauphinois / Creamy potato gratin

Lyonnaise potatoes

The Bistro Starters and Desert menu

The Bistro (Café/Diner)

Starters

Pastry
Tartlettes aux champignons de bias / Mushrooms on pastry *(Pate feuilletee)*

Tarte au Chevre / Goats cheese tart

Soup
Soupe gratinee a l'oigion / French onion soup

Salad
Salade de Pommes de terre / Potato salad
Salade Printaniere / Bacon, lettuce, Tomato, Runner beans, Poached egg
Carottes rapees au mile / Sweet spicy carrots

Dressing
Aioli Marseille
Mayonnaise
Rouille
Vinaigrette aux herbes
Anchovy vinaigrette

Dessert
Mausse au chocolate / Chocolate mouse

Fruit
Peches cardinal au coulis de framboise / Peaches with raspberry sauce

Cheese
Selection of Cheeses

The Bistro (Café/Diner) Beverage Menu
The Bistro (Café/Diner)

HOT

Espresso

Latte

Cappuccino

Americano

Macchiato

Ristretto

Scottish tea

Green Tea

Water Still- Sparkling

JUICE

Orange

Apple

Grape

Cranberry

CANNED

Cola

Orange

Lemonade

Diet

The Bistro Profit and Loss summary

The Bistro (Café/Diner) Profit and Loss Summary

	TOTAL
Sales	
Breakfast	6,000
Solutions	25,000
Totals	51,800
	-
	-
Gross Profit	51,800
	-
Overheads	-
Sales Costs	6,000
Admin Costs	380
Building Costs	16,807
Finance Costs	3,027
	-
Totals	26,214
Net Profit/Loss	25,586
	-
Cumulative	153,610

The Bistro (Café/Diner) Summary Financial Sheet

	Jan	Feb	Mar	Apr	May	Jun	Jul	Aug	Sep	Oct	Nov	Dec	TOTAL
Sales													
Breakfast	500	500	500	500	500	500	500	500	500	500	500	500	6,000
Solutions	2,000	2,000	2,000	2,000	2,000	2,000	2,000	2,000	2,000	2,000	2,500	2,500	25,000
Totals	4,000	4,000	4,000	4,200	4,200	4,200	4,200	4,200	4,200	4,200	5,200	5,200	51,800
Gross Profit	4,000	4,000	4,000	4,200	4,200	4,200	4,200	4,200	4,200	4,200	5,200	5,200	51,800
Overheads													
Sales Costs	500	500	500	500	500	500	500	500	500	500	500	500	6,000
Admin Costs	32	32	32	32	32	32	32	32	32	32	32	32	380
Building Costs	1,401	1,401	1,401	1,401	1,401	1,401	1,401	1,401	1,401	1,401	1,401	1,401	16,807
Finance Costs	252	252	252	252	252	252	252	252	252	252	252	252	3,027
Totals	2,184	2,184	2,184	2,184	2,184	2,184	2,184	2,184	2,184	2,184	2,184	2,184	26,214
Net Profit/Loss	1,816	1,816	1,816	2,016	2,016	2,016	2,016	2,016	2,016	2,016	3,016	3,016	25,586
Cumulative	1,816	3,631	5,447	7,462	9,478	11,493	13,509	15,524	17,540	19,555	22,571	25,586	153,610

Your Small Restaurant: The Bistro (Café/Diner) Practical Business Plan

www.ingramcontent.com/pod-product-compliance
Lightning Source LLC
Chambersburg PA
CBHW072231170526
45158CB00002BA/846